BRAIN
BUILDING
Games

GEDDES & GROSSET

This edition published 2010 by Geddes & Grosset
144 Port Dundas Road, Glasgow, G4 0HZ, Scotland

First Published 2001 by Brainwaves Books, a Division of Allen D. Bragdon Publishers, Inc.,
252 Great Western Road, South Yarmouth, MA 02664

Design and editorial production: Carolyn Zellers. Exercise editing: Wallace Exman. Puzzle
graphics formatting: David Zellers. Performance Tips text rewrite: Melissa Pendleton.
Proofreader: Vida Morris

Drawings by Malcolm Wells

This book is the first of two books and contains explanatory material that is common to
both. Some puzzle concepts were first published in a column called " Playspace" that was
created by Allen Bragdon in the 1980s for global syndication by The New York Times.

ISBN 978-1-84205-655-4

Printed in the UK

Contents

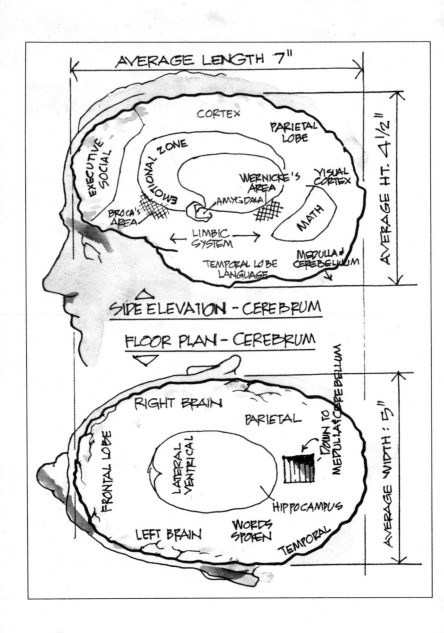

Congratulations! You have decided to take charge of your brain's future. That is the hard part. Our contribution to that effort is to create exercises in interesting puzzle formats. We are also going to tell you how the six cognitive systems that work hardest for you in real-world situations can be made to do their best work. We call these functions the *Executive, Memory, Computation, Spatial, Language* and *Social/Emotional*. Those are the ones that make you excel at work, build a useful store of memories, plan for and live an interesting old age.

Permit us some straight talk about your second most valuable possession. Your brain began to slow down as soon as its original blueprint finished unfolding in your mid-20s. It has lost capacity at the same rate every year since, and it will continue to do so. Symptoms of slowing down — from "senior moments" to Alzheimer's — are simply signs of the cumulative effects of continuing loss that have begun to show up in your outward behaviour.

The good news is that you can *do* something about that. You took the first step when you picked up this book. It is designed to help you slow down the slowing down. There are no pills or vaccines yet to boost your intelligence with no effort. In the future some memory-enhancing pills will be tested, approved and sold. Now, targeted exercise is as good for your brain as for your muscles and cardio-pulmonary systems.

Try one exercise each day. Start with the easy ones. If you get stuck, don't quit on that exercise. Use the "Hint" printed in small type, upside down at the bottom of the page. Rotate from chapter to chapter during each week. Think of that daily routine as being like sets of physical exercises for different muscle-groups. When you have finished the book try one of the first ones you did again. Even if you have forgotten the answer you will be surprised at how easy it seems.

Each day you will be able to learn something about how the human brain works when it solves problems. We call these performance tips "didjaknows" because many of them will come as a surprise. Yet we have selected them from cutting-edge neuroscientific research results, many of them from research published since the millennium. Often you can apply them directly to real life situations to improve performance. Some will confirm a sense you have had all along, on your own, about how the brain gets things done.

Together, the exercises and the performance tips will help you in three, quite different, ways. First, they will make you more effectively aware that you can actually control much of what goes on in your brain. You can improve the hand you were dealt. Second, they will teach you strategies for seeing problems in ways that suggest solutions. The different puzzle formats can be applied to real-world problems. Third, you will be growing stronger brain cells. Yes, when you make cells work they will physically grow new connectors, called *dendrites* and *axons*, that allow them to pass along signals from cell to cell. Like anything else, the more resources you can bring to bear on a problem, the more likely you are to find a good solution.

And speaking of solutions, they are all there in the back of the book. Forget about our solution until you have finished the puzzle *your* way. A major reason for sticking with a puzzle until you have mastered it, painful as it may be, is that it benefits you in the same way "no pain, no gain" does in a physical exercise routine. It builds up the same kind of stamina. It's known as "concentration" in mental performance.

Perseverance can be improved in the same way that aerobic training equips you to run or swim longer and longer each time. Often, superior concentration powers will win a competitive race to a solution.

A few housekeeping points:

We first created most of the puzzle formats in this book of mental exercises for a daily column requested by *The New York Times* to syndicate outside the United States in the 1980s. We called it "Playspace" and meant it. Play is an essential activity to further learning. Consider the most ferociously productive period of learning in your own life. Between the ages of two and six you taught yourself the grammar and vocabulary of a language you had never heard before. You learned the rules of right and wrong in a confused society. You stood up, risked gravity and walked forward. You moved from convenience to duty when you bought into potty training. That's a lot to accomplish in four years. The whole time you were playing, or so it seemed to all those huge people around you who were busy doing important things with their lives. You were really studying them like laboratory animals that fed *you*, picking up clues as fast as your neurons could scamper. Long live a light and eager heart!

For most of our mature lives, David and I have been joyfully engaged in learning how the human brain works its miracles — and devising tasks for it. We hope we have chosen well enough to captivate your interest and entertain your neurons while they stretch.

— Allen Bragdon

Section One
EXECUTIVE

The *Executive Function* in the human brain is located in the frontal part of the forehead above the eyes. This area has evolved after the other areas of the primate brain. It is also the last to mature in children and does not fully develop until after the age of nine. Some neurophysiologists even claim it is not fully developed until the early 20s — a view also held by many parents based on their empirical evidence. As in the L.I.F.O. (Last In, First Out) system of inventory management, its accumulated bundle of human skills tends to be the first to deteriorate with age.

Executive thinking tools are comprised of cleverly-designed devices. One such device is *Working Memory* which holds data in mind temporarily while the brain manipulates it. Notice, for example, how you multiply 89 x 91 in your head. Or read the following sentence and answer the question that appears on the next page. "The waitress asked her assistant to clear the blue dishes but leave the bread basket for the bartender to take home to his parrot."

Business executives are, or should be, skilled at visualizing possible future paths for the firm and charting the intermediate steps required to achieve the chosen goal. As new data emerges, the executive must adapt original strategies without sacrificing the goal.

Accordingly, Executive Functions include the capacity to alter responses to adjust to new data. The brain can adapt responses productively as the patterns of incoming data change, while still keeping the original goal in mind. *Einstellung* is the German word used by neuropsychologists to identify a mind set that cannot spot a new trend in a stream of data. Those minds continue to respond in an unproductive manner.

Many of the mental exercises in this section utilize *convergent* logic skills in which the working memory examines the data presented and works out the only correct conclusion. (Data: *Socrates is a man. All men are mortal.* Conclusion: *Socrates is mortal.)*

Divergent Intelligence, on the other hand, equips the mind to spot unfamiliar patterns. Often, they are newly forming within familiar data. It is also processed in the prefrontal area where Executive functions reside. In many senses it is the anthesis of the *Einstellung* mind set. Interestingly, if the frontal area of the brain is damaged, convergent thinking skills are lost but the IQ remains unchanged. On page 92, you will find a game to play with someone else that reveals tendencies to think either inside or outside the envelope, or both. (Who wanted the bread basket?)

As the brain ages, the ability to manipulate data quickly with the Working Memory tool slows down. In fact it begins losing its edge when the brain has become fully mature in the early 20s. The rate of loss stays constant into old age but the cumulative effect commonly does not show up until "senior moments" begin to occur in the 60s.

The good news is that most Executive Function skills can be maintained by using them — working on the mental exercises in this book, for example. Because this galaxy of skills is essential to the highest levels of thinking, of insight and of productive behaviour, they are worth cultivating lifelong to maintain the highest quality of life.

Adam & Eva?

DIRECTIONS

Two ladies with three-letter first names are hiding in this maze of letters. See how many times you can spell out each of their names reading right to left, left to right, top to bottom, bottom to top, and both ways diagonally.

Didjaknow... LEARNING IS HINDERED WHEN THE BRAIN CAN'T SAY "NO"

The deficits of attention deficit hyperactivity disorder (ADHD) are associated more with faulty output functions of the brain than the brain's intake functions. Recent research indicates that ADHD is not so much an "attention" disorder as an inhibition that leads to *intentional* disorder; the child's consciousness cannot filter out random data that is unproductive, so it acts on everything. Inhibition is often in conflict with intention, and an essential component of the brain's Executive Function is to just say "no" to unproductive impulses that interfere with achieving a desired goal. If the brain is not able to shut off impulses, negative consequences often result: intake, learning, and goals may not be attained.

Answer on page 107

The Able Accountant

Tom and Dick, their cousin Harry, and Jim the greengrocer have shared an accountant, Able, for the past few months. They are pleased with his work and are planning to surprise him with a salary increase at the end of four months, but can't agree when that would be. The discussion is taking place on the weekend — away from the stores where their records are kept. It goes as follows:

Tom: Able came to us at the end of December or the first of January.

Dick: My recollection is of a heavy snowstorm the week he started and I know we sold 15 snow shovels the first week in February.

Answer on page 107

Harry: No. We hired him quite a while after I opened my drug and vitamin business, which I think was about January 12th. He might have started in March.

Jim: His four months will be up in May or June.

Which statement could be correct?

Didjaknow... **STRESS HORMONES MIGHT HELP OR MIGHT HURT**

People would not survive without the production of the stress hormone adrenaline or cortisol. These hormones give humans the ability to react and respond. They essentially provide protection and adaptation in relation to life events. When people are new at public speaking, they often experience an increase in adrenaline and cortisol, and in turn, blood pressure and heart rate increases. After several speeches, adrenaline continues to rise, which is needed to give a speaker "the edge", but cortisol levels usually do not.

Cortisol affects almost all body functions: it has a direct influence on the receptors in a cell's nucleus, regulates metabolism in the liver and aspects of brain function, and affects the immune system, cardiovascular function, heart rate, and blood pressure. While stress hormones are needed for survival, prolonged increases of cortisol can have a negative influence and accelerate certain disease processes.

HINT: Who's guessing and who isn't?

Thirty-Four All

DIRECTIONS

Using all the numbers 5 to 16 only once, make a magic square in which the sum of the numbers you insert in the boxes will be the same horizontally, vertically, and along each diagonal. In this case 34 is the magic number.

Didjaknow... "EXECUTIVE" IS AMONG THE MOST RECENTLY-EVOLVED FUNCTIONS

The Executive Functions which evolved in the most anterior (forward) part of the human brain just above the eyebrow, perform the most uniquely human cognitive tasks. These include planning behaviour and control of instinctive responses to achieve goals set for the future. The Executive Function interprets current data for its value in time-future. It also coordinates sophisticated physical movements such as those needed to speak words. Prefrontal skills are located in two areas of the brain: *Prefrontal cortex*, the outer surface of the front sides, and *orbital frontal* regions, from the front centre point deep down to the brain's interior.

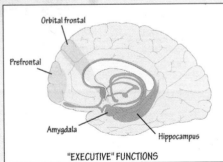

Orbital frontal
Prefrontal
Amygdala
Hippocampus
"EXECUTIVE" FUNCTIONS

There, it links with the more primitive, *limbic* systems including the *hippocampus* (helps route data into memory) and *amygdala* (keeps alert for crucial new data).

Answer on page 107

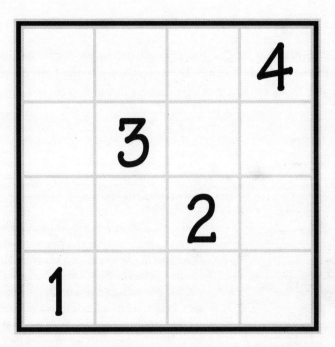

The Square Rooter

DIRECTIONS

Each horizontal row in the grid on the facing page has the same mathematical relationship. If you can identify the pattern, you will be able to supply the missing numbers in the bottom row.

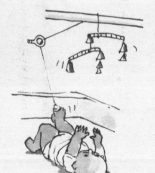

Didjaknow...

INFANTS LIKE TO TAKE ACTION

Although a human needs to be at least six years of age to *imagine* the cause and effect of a sequence of events, an infant quickly learns to repeat a physical movement that produces an obvious reward. If a string is attached from an infant's toe to a visible mobile, an infant quickly catches on that each time he kicks his leg the mobile will move. This action will be repeated to the delight and fascination of the infant. To keep an infant occupied while you go about your duties, set him up with toys that provide a direct, physical connection between action and reward.

Answer on page 107

1	9	6	1	4
3	6	1	1	9
2	8	9	1	7
2	5	6	1	6
3	2	4	?	?

HINT: Work horizontally row by row, first with the first three numbers, then with the last two.

The Angry*!$%?Typist

DIRECTIONS

Each symbol represents a digit, and always the same digit. Double symbols represent two-digit numbers. The asterisk represents an arithmetical sign, but not necessarily the same sign in each equation. Try to figure out the values of the symbols. Yes, the answers are all the same number.

Didjaknow... HAVING TO DEAL WITH UNFAMILIAR DATA KEEPS BRAINS YOUNG

Interestingly, older university professors tested in Executive Function skills, which include Working Memory tasks, score higher than people of the same age who have followed other walks of life. Their scores on such tests are more competitive with test scores of young graduate students. Coping with change such as new students each year, new discoveries in their chosen fields and changing administrative policies may be the causative factors.

Answer on page 107

		&	!	*	?	@	=	•	#
		"	*	@	*	?	=	•	#
		¢	*	¢	*	#	=	•	#
	"	*	¢	*	!	•	=	•	#
&	"	*	&	*	!	=	•	#	
(	(	*	!	¢	*	•	=	•	#

HINT: *The exclamation point is a one and the question mark is a three.*

CITATIONS

P. 12 Denckla, Martha Bridge, MD, Director, Developmental Cognitive Neurology, The Johns Hopkins School of Medicine. From a presentation at Science of Cognition Conference, Library of Congress, Washington, D.C., 6 Oct. 1999.

P. 15 McEwen, Bruce PhD, Head of Hatch Laboratory of Neuroendocrinology, Rockefeller University. From a presentation at Science of Cognition Conference, Library of Congress, Washington, D.C., 6 Oct. 1999.

P. 16 Gazzaniga, M. et al. (1998). Cognitive Neuroscience, W.W. Norton, New York.

P. 18 Diamond, Adele. "Learning and the Brain" Conference. (1999) Boston, MA.

Section Two
MEMORY

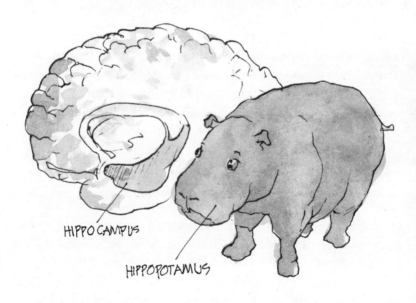

HIPPOCAMPUS

HIPPOPOTAMUS

This is about memory(s), plural, because the brain uses many different strategies to store data, retrieve it and distort it. If you know something about how these systems work you can tap the brain's built-in memory systems strategies to devise the best strategy each time.

Explicit memory (sometimes called *declarative* memory) is the kind you use when you consciously make an effort to remember something. Your brain stores *implicit, nondeclarative*, memories without your even knowing it has happened, much less being aware of trying. That is how you learned your native language, for example.

Here are two strategies for converting new data into long term explicit memory. Repeat the data in different ways: write it down, say it aloud, explain it to someone else, diagram it. Let it rest a while, then go over it again. Spacing out those rehearsal sessions will help.

Another method of learning new data is to steal a trick from your implicit memory system. Your implicit memory of an event (called *episodic* memory) becomes permanent because it was emotionally charged — your wedding day, an accident or the name of your first lover, for example. Often you can artificially apply an emotional "tag" to otherwise dull facts by associating them with some other weird or dramatic memory.

Relate all new data to existing memories. The more familiar hooks you hang a new fact on the more likely you will be able to recall it. Why? Your memory of something that happened to you is stored in many different parts of your brain. The smells of it in one place, the colours, the touch sensations, the sounds of it all in different arrays of cells. When you recall it, any one of those components can trigger the brain to go around and collect all the others to reconstruct the richness of the whole event. When you try to commit a description of an "event" to memory, say a date in history or a list of criteria for a diagnosis, create as many possible "triggers" as you can by visualizing the "event" in association with many different senses and familiar places or other events.

Strategies are important if you want to improve memory skills because practice does not help. Where practice does help is to lengthen the time you can concentrate on a task, much as you can build lung capacity, then stamina, with aerobic exercise. The short answer to building up the ability to focus longer is to force yourself to stay with a task. So don't put down the puzzle the first time you hit a wall working it. Pause, if you like, to think a minute, but don't quit. If you are stuck, look at the hint printed upside down to get going again. Every time you don't quit you build the capacity to stick with it longer, if only a little. The effect is cumulative and worth the effort. If you can't concentrate you can't develop the *explicit* memory strategies you will need to enter new data into memory.

Beware of false memory. True memory can easily become distorted when you recall it. The brain organizes the vast store of data it must recall by piecing it back together in ways that follow other past experience. When details are missing, it tries to insert what "must" have happened. It will also fill in details that are suggested to it by the way a question is posed when you are asked to recall something.

Why you forget also reveals something about why you remember. When two bunches of data command your attention in sequence, such as when you read two stories in an anthology, your memory of details of the first will dim for a while, a natural occurrence called *retroactive inhibition*. That is why people sometimes find themselves in a place but can't recall what they went there for. Usually it is because something interesting commanded their attention on the way there.

The Early Early Bird

Natalie Nuthatch knew she'd have the pick of the crop at a local car boot sale if she arrived early enough, but on this particular Saturday morning she arrived before the setting-up preparations had been completed. Asked to come back at the appointed hour, a chastened Natalie made a surreptitious inventory of the items already on display at her favourite spot before beating a retreat and, upon returning at the proper time, quickly noted the items that had been added during her absence. Study the array of objects that Natalie first observed in the top picture, then turn the page upside-down and examine the objects in the lower picture that she found upon her return. Without looking back at the first picture, can you tell which items had been added to the sale?

Didjaknow... MEMORY IS THE MOTHER OF ALL FUNCTIONS

When anything goes wrong with the brain, the first system affected is memory. Any fluctuation in mental state, such as depression, anxiety, or stress, will have a negative impact on the brain's memory system. Following a brain injury, memory is almost always the first thing that goes. Damage to the parietal and temporal parts on the left side of the brain is most likely to affect language memory since the left hemisphere specializes in language, verbal, and analytic processes. The right hemisphere specializes in spatial, facial, more Gestalt processes; damage to this side is more likely to affect spatial reasoning and spatial memory.

Answer on page 108

Circles Within Circles

DIRECTIONS

This exercise works your brain in circles. The heavily circled number 1 is surrounded by six other numbers — all different. Search the vase for nine additional similar combinations: a number surrounded by six other numbers, none of which is alike.

Didjaknow... THE SOUND OF LANGUAGE IS IMPORTANT FOR COMPREHENSION

The brain uses special tricks to discriminate and translate fast-moving spoken syllables into meaningful words and to convert patterns of letters on a printed page into meaningful spoken words. In both cases, the ability to hold sounds in short-term "working" memory is crucial.

To understand the meaning of any sentence, the brain must hold in memory the idea started by the words in the first part of the sentence while the eyes or ears are taking in the words in the last part of the sentence — just as you did when you read this one. If a child who is learning to read, can also hear the words in his "mind's ear", he can hold in memory the sound of the beginning of the sentence long enough to add meaning to what the second half of the sentence expresses.

Answer on page 108

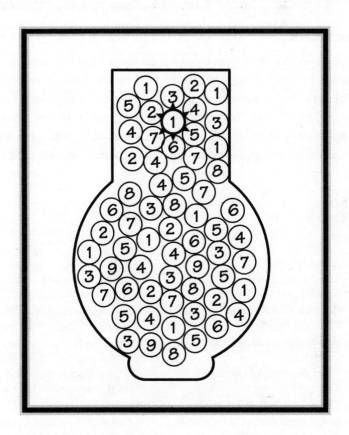

HINT: Start with number 1 in the second circle from the bottom.

The French Connection

DIRECTIONS

Solve this puzzle as you would a crossword puzzle using numbers instead of words. Only the digits 1 to 9 are used; there are no zeros. Only one digit may be placed in each box, and a digit may be used more than once in an answer. Where it appears that more than one combination of digits is possible, look for additional clues in the interlocking answers. A prime number is divisible only by itself and 1.

CLUES

ACROSS

1. The beginning of the French Revolution
4. A prime number
5. The Arabic number denoting which Louis was in power at the time of 1 Across
7. 17—, the execution of Revolutionary leader Georges Danton
8. 17—, the birth of painter Corot
9. The month and day in 1793 of the execution of 5 Across; the square of a prime number
10. Birth year of painter Delacroix

DOWN

1. The end of the French Revolution; birth year of novelist Balzac
2. Bastille Day (month and day)
3. An odd number; the sum of the second and fourth digits is one-third of each of the other digits
6. An even number; each of the first two digits is three less than the sum of the last two digits
9. A prime number that is also the reverse of 4 Across

Answer on page 108

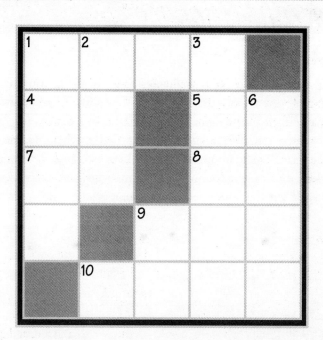

Didjaknow... **LONG TERM STRESS HURTS THE HIPPO (AND MEMORY)**

Long-term stress can harm a part of the brain called the hippocampus. The hippocampus contains receptors for the stress hormone cortisol and repeated increases of cortisol can impair declarative memory. The hippocampus can withstand short-term stress, but if stress is long-term, results are more negative. The hippocampus in people with recurrent depressive illness becomes 10-12 percent smaller in volume.

HINT: The sum of 9 Across is 4.

Heavenly Harmonies

DIRECTIONS

The answers to the clues are names. Choose a letter that appears at least once anywhere in the full name. The correct letter must appear as many times in the name as the available number of boxes allotted for each clue number, reading *across* only. (For example, the correct name for 13 would allow either two As or two Hs.) When correctly chosen, each row across will repeat the same letter. Every column will spell out the same theme-word appropriate to this puzzle.

CLUES

1. Jazz trumpeter (1926-1991)
2. *South Pacific* star (1913-1990)
3. American dancer and choreographer (1894-1991)
4. Jazz pianist (1920-1982)
5. Austrian composer (1797-1828)
6. French composer (1862-1918)
7. Austrian waltz composer (1825- 1899)
8. American composer (1896-1985)
9. Violin superstar (1901-1987)
10. *West Side Story* composer (1918-1990)
11. *William Tell* composer (1792-1868)
12. Opera superstar (1873-1921)
13. "Stardust" composer (1899-1981)
14. *Appalachian Spring* composer (1900-1990)

Answer on page 108

1	2		3	
4	5	6		7
8				9
10	11			
12		13		14

Didjaknow...

MORE BRAIN, MORE MEMORY GAINED

The more the brain encodes, the better the memory. Subjects were given memorizing tasks: lists of words; sets of unfamiliar faces; and sets of nameable pictures such as a line-drawn dog. The brain's left dorsal frontal region memorizes word lists (verbal), while unfamiliar faces require the right prefrontal brain (nonverbal). Because nameable pictures use both sides of the brain (two codes), they were remembered best.

HINT: 13 is Hoagy Carmichael.

CITATIONS

P. 26 Gur, Ruben C. PhD. Sex Differences in Learning. Using Brain Research to
    Reshape Classroom Practice. From a presentation at the Learning and the Brain
    Conference. Boston, MA, 7-9 Nov. 1999.

P. 28 Eden, Guinevere D.Phil., Georgetown University Medical Center. From a
    presentation at Science of Cognition Conference, Library of Congress,
    Washington, D.C., 6 Oct. 1999.

P. 31 McEwen, Bruce PhD., Head of the Hatch Laboratory of Neuroendocrinology,
    Rockefeller University. From a presentation at Science of Cognition
    Conference, Library of Congress, Washington, D.C., 6 Oct. 1999.

P. 32 Park, Denise PhD. The Center for Applied Cognitive Research on Aging,
    University of Michigan. From a presentation at the Science of Cognition
    Conference. Library of Congress, Washington, D.C., 6 Oct. 1999.

Section Three
COMPUTATION

What part of your brain will you be exercising as you work on the tasks in the Computation section? Many researchers believe there are different information-processing styles associated with each of your brain's hemispheres. The left is analytic, linear, serial-processing; it sees every tree in the forest, laboriously analysing and inspecting each in turn. The right is synthetic, simultaneous, parallel-processing; it quickly sizes up the shape and texture of the forest as a whole.

Language and maths may seem to be strictly linear, hence left-brain, skills. Both manipulate units of sound and sight (phonemes, syllables, digits and symbols) that can be combined in many ways according to rules. However, complex problem-solving skills like those must draw on systems in both hemispheres. For example, the flash of insight that led Einstein to his theory of relativity occurred as he considered the moving hands of the town-hall clock through the window of the moving tram on the way to work. That time-space insight was right-brain. The painstaking process of translating that insight into numbers was left-brain.

Two of the puzzle formats in this section are a lot like crossword puzzles with numbers rather than words. The interlocking answers to the clues help eliminate incorrect responses. The strategy is to fill in obvious answers as extra clues to pare down possibilities for the others. Take a look at the simplified fragment on the facing page, for example. If you look at each clue in turn, you'll see that every one suggests multiple solutions. Any line of boxes, taken alone, could be filled in with any of several answers, but only some of those answers could be compatible with the clues given for intersecting lines of boxes.

Clues:

1 Across	13 x 1, 2, or 3
3 Across	A palindrome; the first digit is the square root of the last two
2 Down	A square

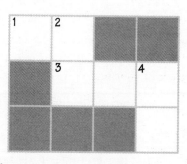

For example, 1 Across could be 13, 26, or 39 and 2 Down could be 16, 25, 36, 49, 64, or 81. But since the second digit of 1 Across is also the first digit of 2 Down, the latter could only be 36 or 64.

So 3 Across must begin with 6 or 4. Let's say it begins with 6. Since the answer must be a palindrome (a number that reads the same forwards and backwards), and the first digit must be the square root of the last two, the answer could be 636. What about the other possibility? If 3 Across begins with 4, then the next two digits would have to be 16 by the square root requirement — but then, it wouldn't be a palindrome. So 3 Across must be 636, 2 Down must be 36, 1 Across must be 13.

To review a few terms: A "square" of any number (say 3) is the number you get when you multiply it by itself (9). The "square root" is the number you started with (3). A "cube" results from multiplying that answer again by itself (81). A "prime" number is any one that cannot be divided evenly except by 1 and itself (For example, 3 or 7 are , but not 6 or 21). "Digits" are the basic numbers in a system or set. In our decimal system they are 0 to 10; in binary system code they are 0 and 1. "Integers" are the numbers you say when you count. Have fun!

Add-Venture Plus

DIRECTIONS

Solve this puzzle as you would a crossword puzzle, using interlocking numbers instead of words. Write a single digit in each box so that the sum of the digits equals the total given for that row or column in the Across and Down clues. For example, the sum of the digits in the 1-Across boxes must total 13. No number is used more than once in any answer, and zero is not used. The digits already in place are correct, so use them as checkpoints to help get started.

Didjaknow... USE MATHS, DON'T LOSE IT

While language skills tend to improve with age, the ability swiftly to perform complex number problems declines. Even expert mathematicians will experience this age-related decline in performance. However, it is possible to slow age-related declines in mathematical performance by exercising maths circuits. For example, work number puzzles, compose mathematical equations to express a problem, estimate your cheque book balance in your head or add up the total cost of your grocery bill while waiting in the checkout line.

Answer on page 109

1
6
2
3
4
5
6
7
8
9
4
10
11
2
4
12
2
13
14
15
16
17
18

CLUES

ACROSS

1. 13
3. 13
5. 22
8. 8
10. 17
11. 15
12. 11
13. 12
15. 17
17. 13
18. 12

DOWN

2. 16
3. 15
4. 5
6. 16
7. 15
9. 13
10. 20
12. 9
14. 8
15. 14
16. 16

HINT: *All the numbers in the rows and columns end with odd digits.*

Addendum & Eve?

DIRECTIONS

Solve this puzzle as you would a crossword puzzle, using interlocking numbers instead of words. Write a single digit in each box so that the sum of the digits equals the total given for that row or column in the Across and Down clues. For example, the sum of the digits in the 1-Across boxes must total 5. No number is used more than once in any answer, and zero is not used. Use the four correct digits already entered as checkpoints to help get started on the right foot.

Didjaknow... WHAT PARTS OF THE BRAIN LIGHT UP WHEN DOING MATHS IN YOUR HEAD?

Simple maths gets done in the *left angular gyrus* and the *medial parietal cortices* which process numerical representations during exact calculation and retrieve arithmetical facts from memory. More complex calculation tasks involving the application of rules, use the *left inferior frontal* areas, also used for language and for Working Memory (the kind used when say, multiplying 89 by 91 in your head, in which some data must be held in mind while other, but related, data is processed).

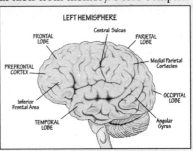

Answer on page 109

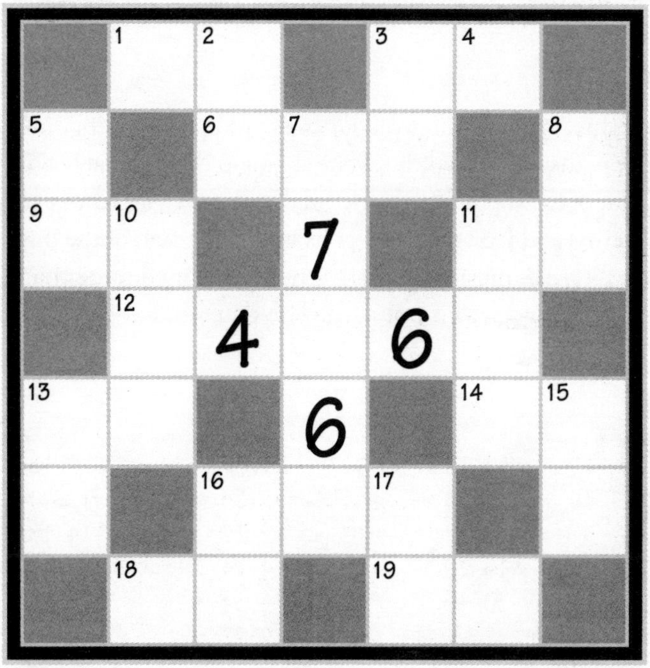

CLUES

ACROSS:

1. 5
3. 5
6. 23
9. 14
11. 17
12. 26
13. 15
14. 8
16. 18
18. 17
19. 12

DOWN

2. 12
3. 9
5. 13
7. 35
8. 15
10. 17
11. 23
13. 13
15. 10
16. 12
17. 14

HINT: *All the numbers in the rows and columns end with even digits.*

Addictive Pleasures

DIRECTIONS

Solve this puzzle as you would a crossword puzzle, using interlocking numbers instead of words. Write a single digit in each box so that the sum of the digits equals the total given for that row or column in the Across and Down clues. For example, the sum of the digits in the 1-Across boxes must total 35. No number is used more than once in any answer, and zero is not used. The entered numbers are correct.

CLUES

ACROSS		DOWN	
1. 35	13. 13	1. 20	9. 18
5. 15	15. 24	2. 26	12. 23
6. 20	17. 22	3. 17	14. 18
8. 30	19. 20	4. 24	16. 15
10. 12	20. 30	5. 34	18. 16
11. 20		7. 32	

Didjaknow... **LEFT-BRAIN DAMAGE MAY INTERFERE WITH COMPUTATION**

Left-brain damage can sometimes cause a condition referred to as *acalculia*. Patients suffering from acalculia are often able to give an answer to an easy, rote-memorized mathematical problem, such as 3 + 3 = 6. However, if the problem is complex and involves computation, such as 13 + 43, these patients will lack the ability to calculate and answer.

Answer on page 109

Tot Up & Tally Ho!

DIRECTIONS

Solve this puzzle as you would a crossword puzzle, using interlocking numbers instead of words. Write a single digit in each box so that the sum of the digits equals the total given for that row or column in the Across and Down clues. For example, the sum of the digits in the 1-Across boxes must total 30. No number is used more than once in any answer, and zero is not used. We have entered a few correct digits to get you started.

CLUES

ACROSS		DOWN	
1. 30	12. 20	1. 32	10. 10
6. 20	13. 15	2. 16	13. 23
7. 13	15. 15	3. 13	14. 19
8. 14	16. 15	4. 25	16. 15
9. 11	17. 29	5. 13	
11. 8		7. 18	

Didjaknow... **NEWBORNS PERCEIVE DIFFERENCE IN QUANTITIES ONLY UP TO 3 OR 4**

An infant seems to detect differences in numerical quantity. When a newborn is shown a picture of 3 dots, he becomes attentive. After repeatedly seeing the picture, he acts indifferent (habituates). Changing the number of dots arouses his interest again provided they range from 1-3 (sometimes 4). Newborns cannot discriminate differences above 3 or 4 so they do not respond. Those higher counts are too much for a newborn's brain to process until many months later in its development.

Answer on page 109

Square Dances

DIRECTIONS

Solve this puzzle as you would a crossword puzzle using numbers instead of words. Only the digits 1 to 9 are used; there are no zeros. Only one digit may be placed in each box, and a digit may be used more than once in an answer. Where it appears that more than one combination of digits is possible, look for additional clues in the interlocking answers. A prime number is divisible only by itself and 1.

CLUES

ACROSS
1. The square of a square (odd)
3. Consecutive digits
5. Consecutive digits out of order
7. Even digits, all different
8. Twelve times a prime number
9. The product of two prime numbers
10. The square of the cube root of 6 down

DOWN
1. A multiple of the square root of 10 Across
2. The sum of the first and third digits is equal to the fourth digit; the second and fifth digits are the same
3. A palindrome of even numbers
4. The cube of a cube (even)
6. A palindrome that is the cube of a prime number
8. A trombone number

Didjaknow... **"CHUNKING" HELPS NUMBER RECALL**

Most people cannot recall a long series of numbers accurately. The answer is to group two- or three-digit sequences into "chunks".

Answer on page 109

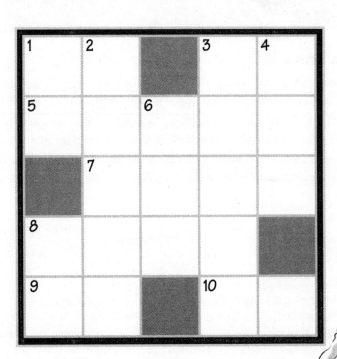

For example, when holding a 10-digit phone number in mind long enough to dial it most people have to group and separate the area code and may combine the remaining single digits into two-digit numbers (6,1,0 as six-ten).

HINT: 1 Across is 81

Prime Time

DIRECTIONS

Solve this puzzle as you would a crossword puzzle using numbers instead of words. Only the digits 1 to 9 are used; there are no zeros. Only one digit may be placed in each box, and a digit may be used more than once in an answer. Where it appears that more than one combination of digits is possible, look for additional clues in the interlocking answers. A prime number is divisible only by itself and 1.

CLUES

ACROSS

1. The square of the third smallest prime number
3. The square of an Arabic number that looks like a Roman 2
4. An odd number that is 30 less than it would be upside down
6. Onion Market Day in Bern, Switzerland
8. The square of a prime number larger than 1 Across and smaller than 3 Across
9. The next square after 8 Across

DOWN

1. The sum of the last two digits equals the sum of the first three
2. The second and fourth digits are alike
3. The square of an even number that itself is a square
5. The next square after 3 Across
7. The sum of its digits is the square root of 9 Across

Answer on page 109

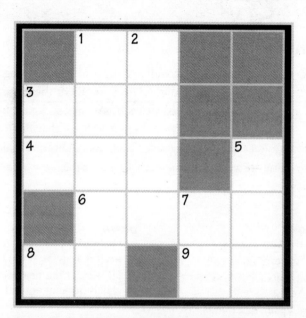

Didjaknow...

A good night's sleep is important for high performance mathematical brain functioning. When maths graduates were awakened from recovery sleep after staying up for 48-hours straight, they were unable to calculate even simple maths problems. The brain needs adequate sleep in order to compute and answer number equations accurately.

HINT: 6 Across is 1124.

Root Causes

DIRECTIONS

Solve this puzzle as you would a crossword puzzle using numbers instead of words. Only the digits 1 to 9 are used; there are no zeros. Only one digit may be placed in each box, and a digit may be used more than once in an answer. Where it appears that more than one combination of digits is possible, look for additional clues in the interlocking answers. A prime number is divisible only by itself and 1.

CLUES

ACROSS
1. Consecutive digits
5. A "variety" number
6. The sum of 1 Across and 9 Across
8. The square of a number that itself is a square (even)
9. The reverse of 1 Across

DOWN
2. The square of a number that itself is a square (even)
3. The sum of the first two digits equals the sum of the last three
4. The sum of the first two digits equals the last digit
6. The square of the number that itself is a square (odd)
7. A number divisible by 2 but not by 4

Answer on page 109

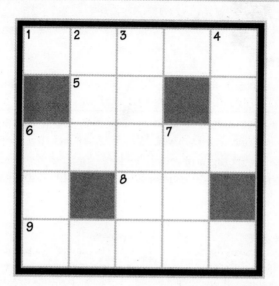

Didjaknow... SAVANTS MAY SUFFER FROM RIGHT-BRAIN DEFICIT

People with one rare ability but low tested IQs typically score low on tests of general intelligence, which tend to favour left-hemisphere skills such as language comprehension, but they do show one extraordinary ability. It is a calculation skill that appears to be mathematical but may be visual. They can quickly tell you what day any given future date will fall on. A study of a pair of twin savants who could tell the day of the week for any date going back over a span of 8,000 years suggested that they may suffer a left-brain dysfunction that forces areas of their right, more visuospatial, hemispheres to take over.

HINT: 5 Across is 57.

Calculated Surprises

DIRECTIONS

Solve this puzzle as you would a crossword puzzle using numbers instead of words. Only the digits 1 to 9 are used; there are no zeros. Only one digit may be placed in each box, and a digit may be used more than once in an answer. Where it appears that more than one combination of digits is possible, look for additional clues in the interlocking answers. A prime number is divisible only by itself and 1.

CLUES

ACROSS

1. The first year in the second half of the 18th century
4. The symmetrical square of an even number
6. The square of an odd number that itself is a square
7. Half of the largest common factor of 3 Down
8. The sum of the fourth and fifth digits is half the square root of 4 Across; the first three are unities
10. The square of an even number that is one more than the square root of 1 Down

DOWN

1. The square of a prime number whose root is one less than the square root of 10 Across
2. The first two digits are a multiple of the last two
3. Consecutive digits
5. The square of an even number that is four less than the square root of 1 Across
7. The square of 7 Across
9. A prime number

Answer on page 109

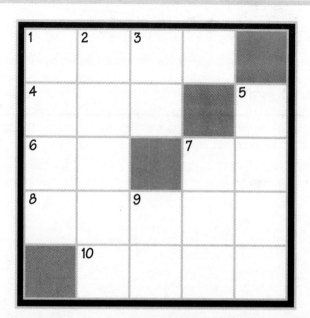

Didjaknow...
NUMBER AND LANGUAGE SKILLS ARE INTERDEPENDENT

Mathematical ability is dependent on language skills in order to name numbers and maths formulations. However, language and computation tasks are processed in different areas of the brain. Documented studies have been made of brain-damaged people who can calculate accurately but are not able to name the numbers or operations used in calculation. On the other hand, there are brain-damaged people who can name numbers and count but lack the ability to calculate and answer mathematical problems.

HINT: 1 Across is 1751.

CITATIONS

P. 38 Bragdon, A., Gamon, D. (2001) The Brainwaves Center, Bass River, MA.

P. 40 O. Gruber, P. Indefrey, H. Steinmetz, and A. Kleinschmidt.
Cerebral Cortex 2001;11 350-359

P. 42-53 Bragdon, A., Gamon, D. (2001) The Brainwaves Center, Bass River, MA.

Section Four
SPATIAL

Visuospatial scratchpad is the term neuroscientists use to refer to a Working Memory tool you will be using when you tackle tasks like the mental exercises on the following pages. Some of the exercises require you to visualize forms in space as architects, builders, sculptors and chess masters must do. In everyday life people use this skill to, for example, fit suitcases into a car's boot or find their way back to the entrance of a building or relocate their car in the shopping centre parking lot.

The right hemisphere of most male brains is more highly specialized for that kind of skill than the female brain normally is. This is one of the most obvious gender differences in cognitive processing and it seems to correlate with what is known about how protohuman primates lived when their brains were evolving 60 million years ago. Women find their way by identifying landmarks. Men are more likely to orient themselves to large geographical reference points, including the sun and stars. It is tempting to speculate that, as hunters, males travelled long distances drawn by game into unfamiliar territory. Women, who kept close to their dwelling to care for infants and to escape predators, would have been more likely to rely on local landmarks to move around seeking food or firewood in familiar territory near their dwelling.

The visuospatial skills can be developed with practice. A recent neuroscientific study of experienced, professional taxi drivers in London, who are required to pass rigorous tests in finding addresses anywhere in the city before they are licensed, showed that a portion of their brain was significantly larger than that of London workers in other jobs. It is called the *hippocampus*, based on the latin word for horse (as hippopotamus also is) because at one time somebody must have thought that organ and animal each looked like a horse (which they don't at all). Every brain has one on each side. The one on the right side, where visuospatial skills are located for most people, was larger in the London cabbies' brains. The neurons in the rear part of that area had sent out more connections to respond to the daily performance demanded of them. This forced an increase in mass which is clearly noticeable in a brain scan.

That finding is a persuasive example of a fact that is little known but is very encouraging. The human brain is able to adapt physically to meet demands put to it, much as a society can change its values in a common crisis or a flower will grow toward the sun's light. This means that the brain responds as other physical systems do. Aerobic exercise builds strength in the heart muscle and oxygen-carrying capacity in the lungs, thereby increasing stamina. Muscle groups gain mass when they are subjected to the regular stresses of targeted exercises. Lifting and running capacity increase as a result. Even if a system has not been used for many years, its mass and effectiveness can be revived with exercise which, incidentally, shows up dramatically in older people who start exercising after leading relatively sedentary lives.

Like life, there is a downside. In the Middle Ages the crafts of architecture, building and draughtsmanship — all trades that target the visuospatial centres in the right hemisphere — were known as the melancholy arts because they were thought to depress the spirit. In fact, the right hemisphere does process negative facial expressions and is more active in the depressed phase of a manic-depressive cycle. But that didn't stop Leonardo da Vinci, nor should it you.

Circling The Square

How an individual observes the world visually has more to do with one's ability to notice shapes, shadows and colours than it does with one's personal preferences. Exposure early in life to specific visual experiences — a quilt on a crib, for example — can affect adult taste profoundly, as do social influences such as advertising and peer group choices. The inexperienced eye of a child lacks the invasive social influences that might subconsciously cloud his vision and alter his choices. The part of the right hemisphere that processes abstract, metaphorical associations tends to weaken with age. Individuals with advanced dementia probably would not perceive the social point of the drawing, on the facing page. Can you?

Didjaknow... SEX HORMONES AFFECT THE BRAIN

While male and female brains are different from birth, the hormones of adolescence seem to increase and magnify the differences. Males tend to decline in verbal ability as they go through puberty, whereas females decline in spatial ability. According to Jean Piaget, everyone by the age of 13 should be able to guess the correct answer to his water level test. Interestingly, girls who knew the correct answer to Piaget's water level test at age 11 often lost the answer by age 13 after starting puberty. The only explanation for these changes is that sex hormones produced at adolescence affect both the body and the brain.

Answer on page 110

HINT: Why is the father showing disapproval of the boy's drawing of a curling line?

Draughtboard Square

DIRECTIONS

Think of a 6 x 6 square, or draw one. How many ways can you place 12 draughts, one to a square, so that each row, column, and the two diagonals contain only two draughts?

Didjaknow... MEN ARE BETTER IN SPATIAL ABILITY

Overall results prove that men do better than women on problems involving spatial reasoning and spatial memory. On line orientation tests, where two lines are shown (each set of lines getting shorter) and one must guess if the lines have the same orientation as another set, a man is most likely to guess the correct answer. Piaget's water level test shows a truck travelling uphill one-half filled with water and asks which line represents the level of water. On this test, 45 percent of men got the answer correct, while only 15 percent of the women did. When the test grew more difficult, involving a rope remaining perpendicular to the ground, 60 percent of the men guessed correctly while only 30 percent of the women did.

Answer on page 110

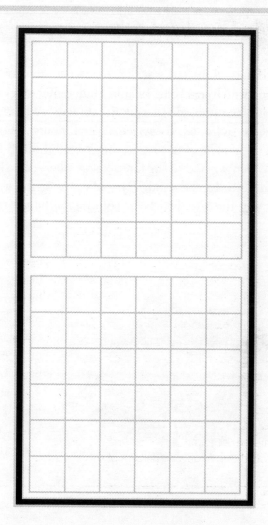

Unexpected Windfall

T he brothers Tom and Dick were invited to Cousin Harry's wedding which was being held in Hurley, 300 miles away. They decided to drive nonstop, alternating the driving. A heavy rainstorm with high winds followed them for several hours. Shortly before sundown, "in the middle of nowhere", they passed through the town of Burley and suddenly came to an intersection where the signpost had been knocked down by the wind. Tom, who was at the wheel, didn't know which way the sign had been pointing, although the town of

Hurley was shown on it. He began berating his brother for not bringing a road map. Dick got out of the car for a few minutes, then got back in and told Tom which road to take. How did he know which way was the correct one?

Answer on page 110

Didjaknow...

EXPLORING NEW AVENUES MAKES THE BRAIN GROW

Here's a new excuse to plan an excursion out of town: exploring new avenues will challenge the brain and literally help it grow. A brain-scan study of London cabbies shows the rear of the hippocampus, a seat of spatial memory, is larger than in other drivers, relative to years of experience. The same area of the hippocampus grows larger in birds forced to learn new navigational or food finding skills. If you've been thinking of finding your way out of town or cross-country, go for it! Travelling that involves mapping out and navigating works your spatial memory.

HINT: Unlike Lot's wife, Tom didn't turn into a pillar of salt.

Topsy-Turvey Tangrams

DIRECTIONS

A tangram is a Chinese puzzle consisting of a square cut into seven pieces — five triangles, a square, and a rhomboid — which then can be combined to form a great variety of figures. The four tangrams, opposite, have been cut from the square in the upper left-hand corner. They are (we think): a vulture (A); a hand-standing acrobat (B); a man wearing a top hat (C); and a raccoon (D). By drawing lines, can you show how each piece in the original square was used to construct each drawing? Identical pieces have the same numbers and are interchangeable in the drawings.

Didjaknow... LESS IS MORE FOR VISUAL STATEMENT

A profile or silhouette often makes a greater visual statement than a colour photograph. For example, mystery writer Alfred Hitchcock was easily recognized from an outline of his face; his particulars such as skin and hair texture were insignificant for his recognition since they were similar to any other person's. Because the visual centres in the brain have limited attention resources, oftentimes a simple drawn outline — which communicates less data — is recognized more quickly than a detailed picture.

Answer on page 110

HINT: The rhomboid (5) is used to form the vulture's tail feathers, the acrobat's upraised hand, the man's nose, and the raccoon's tail.

Twice Burned

DIRECTIONS

It can be said that the 40 matches shown opposite form 16 squares. It can also be said that they form 9 squares made up of four small squares each, 4 squares of nine squares each, and one large square (the perimeter), making a total of 30 squares altogether.

1. What is the least number of matches that can be removed to eliminate all the squares?

2. Using the matches you removed, can you form 6 new squares?l

---

Didjaknow... MEN TAKE TO TRAVEL

When couples are travelling, frequently the man is found in the driver's seat. The reason for this customary seating arrangement may have more

to do with biology than male chivalry. Brain studies show the circuits specialized for path finding are naturally larger in most male brains than female brains. Males tend to navigate by orientation to general geography and directional clues such as the sun. Females tend to use landmarks along the route more often.

Answer on page 110

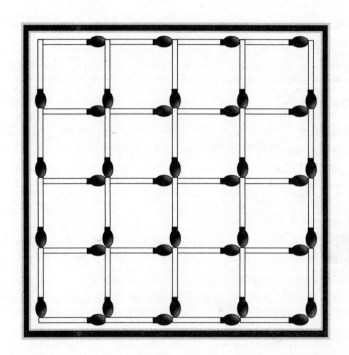

CITATIONS

P. 58 Gur, Ruben C. Sex Differences in Learning. Using Brain Research to Reshape Classroom Practice. Public Information Resources, Inc. 7-9 Nov. 1999.

P. 60 Gur, Ruben C.

P. 63 Maguire, E.A. et al. (2000). Navigation-related structural changes in the hippocampi of taxi drivers. Proceedings of the National Academy of Sciences USA 97/8:4398-403.

P. 64 Ramachandran, V.S. MD, PhD. Professor and Director, Center for Brain and Cognition, University of California-San Diego. From a presentation at the Science of Cognition Conference. Library of Congress. Washington, D. C., 6 Oct. 1999.

P. 66 Maguire, E.A. et al. (2000).

Clayton, N.S., and J.R. Krebs (1994). Hippocampal growth and attrition in birds affected by experience. Proceedings of the National Academy of Sciences USA 91:7410-14.

Section Five
LANGUAGE

Have you heard about the latest brain research? If you stimulate your brain with cognitive challenges, you'll raise its dopamine levels. Dopamine is a neurotransmitter produced by the brain to facilitate passing signals among brain cells. Dopamine also makes you feel good by causing a rewarding sense of satisfaction, especially when the brain works on a left-hemisphere task like a word task. The same stimulus-reward system is activated by some narcotics. Your brain loves to feel good. If it can't do it by solving puzzles, it'll look for other means. The puzzles are generally better for you than the other means that don't add to your vocabulary much.

Consider, just for a moment, how lucky we humans are to be able to learn our language all by ourselves at such an early age that we think life is *supposed* to be that much work. Infants and young children learn the basic structure, pronunciation, grammar and most of the vocabulary of their native language independently of the teaching skills of their parents. Self-education in acquisition of a skill that complex is a stroke of brilliance in brain design. Recruiting a self-motivating neurotransmitter like dopamine as a player in that process is a second masterstroke. Together, they seem to verify that brain design, like the design of a lasting political constitution, requires a realistic appraisal of human motivations and self-interest.

English is trickier than most languages. It is harder to read, write, and spell English words, and make sense of fast-moving conversation and printed paragraphs. The incidence of dyslexia, for example, is lower in non-English-speaking communities. The difference is not schooling, it is the consistency of the language.

The 40-odd sounds in English can be written in over 1,000 different ways. The brain has to work faster to decode English sentences — does that "gh" sound like an "ff" in tough or "gas" in ghastly, or what? In Italian, for example, you get just what you see, every time. The fact that Italy has half as many dyslexic children per capita as the U.S. may be because the human brain can decode the sounds of an Italian sentence milliseconds faster than the same sentence in English. Milliseconds count in processing word comprehension of a new language — a child in preschool could tell you that (as soon as he learns to speak his native tongue, of course).

What part of your brain will you be exercising in this section of the book? Left, mostly. The right side is more active in Sections 4 and 6. Word processing may seem exclusively left-brain linear because you must keep track of sound- and meaning-units produced in rapid sequence. Some aspects of language recall are linear, but not all. You can't "get" verbal jokes or puns unless you hold multiple ideas in your head at once — an ability shared by the front part of both hemispheres, but mostly the right. Incidentally, the burst of laughter that follows a good joke also enlists circuits of stimulus and reward. The stimulus is to search for how the surprising punch line *does* follow the set-up story line. When the punch-line hits, your brain relishes scurrying around to figure out how the unexpected fits. The reward part comes when you "get" it.

We designed these exercises to help you feel good and stay smart. Few other things in life that are so good for you are this much fun.

DIRECTIONS

Rearrange each group of letters to form a different word, then place the new words in the grid, starting each in its numbered square, so that each word reads the same across and down, e.g., 1 Across and 1 Down read the same, 2 Across and 2 Down read the same, etc. Clues to the correct words for all five groups are given in parentheses.

Didjaknow... **LEARNING DISABILITIES ARE DETERMINED BY SOCIETY**

A learning disability is defined as a cognitive function that is disproportionately weak and causes a problem in some activity of daily living. Many people compensate for a functional weakness by using other abilities and, therefore, are never evaluated or diagnosed as having a learning disability. A learning disability is actually defined by the society you are living in. British society does not test for musical ability, for example, because it does not require a citizen to become an accomplished musician. However, reading is considered necessary to function in our society, so those who lack the ability to read need to be evaluated for a possible learning disability.

Answer on page 111

1	2	3	4	5
2				
3				
4				
5				

CLUES

1. PARTS (looped band)
2. RHATS (rubbish)
3. DORIA (British wireless)

4. INASA (Thai, e.g.)
5. YONHP (fake)

HINT: *The answer to 4 is ASIAN.*

Winner-Word

DIRECTIONS

Start at a single letter (E, A, or I) and add a letter to it to spell a two-letter word in the next row. Then add a letter to spell a three-letter word in the third row. Continue until you complete the six-letter word in the sixth row. You may rearrange the letters to spell each new word. Work the centre puzzle from the single letter A to the top, and the other two, from E and I, to the bottom. No proper nouns, abbreviated, hyphenated, or foreign words are allowed. Each letter falling in a circle has the number of points shown in the "letter values" column. When all three diagrams are completed, use any six letters from the three six-letter words and spell out a new six-letter word in the Winner-Word box. Each of these letters is worth DOUBLE their letter value. Then add up your circled-letter points and your Winner-Word points and write your answer in the Total box.

Didjaknow... LEFT BRAIN LIKES FAMILIAR SYMBOLS

While the left hemisphere tends to be verbal and the right hemisphere tends to be visual, these abilities are not completely specialized to one side. Familiar icons and symbols, such as letters of the alphabet or a handicap symbol, are automatically processed by the left-brain. Less familiar visual images, such as a strange face or odd-shaped object, are handled more on the right side of the brain. Even a foreign language that uses unfamiliar symbols, such as the Chinese alphabet, would first be processed by the right brain.

Answer on page 111

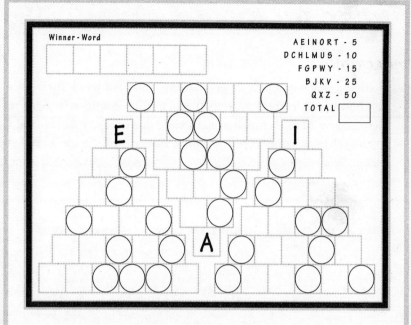

How close can you come to our total?

Within 100 points — Excellent

Within 150 points — Good

Within 200 points — Fair

Within 300 points — Better use a dictionary!

HINT: Our six-letter word at the bottom of the E ladder is DAZZLE.

Erect An Island

DIRECTIONS

Rearrange each group of letters to form a different word, then place the new words in the grid, starting each in its numbered square, so that each word reads the same across and down, e.g., 1 Across and 1 Down read the same, 2 Across and 2 Down read the same, etc. A clue to one correct word in the five groups is given in parentheses.

Didjaknow... "LIKE WHATEVER" HINDERS TEENS

All teenagers develop peer lingo, but if jargon slows vocabulary growth, it may limit the future. The average 14-year-old knows about 20,000 words. If learning continues at this rate, by age 64, the vocabulary will consist of 100,000 words (half of a large dictionary). To achieve this, a teen has to learn approximately 150 new words a month. Asking your adolescent to use alternate words for "like, whatever" forces the developing brain to organize and use information more precisely. Benefits are numerous. Besides building brain power, the increased vocabulary boosts fluidity of verbal expression and reading skills, thus leading to better job prospects. Studies also show that an increased vocabulary may reduce the risk for Alzheimer's.

Answer on page 111

1	2	3	4	5
2				
3				
4				
5				

CLUES

1. ERECT
2. NVEAR (bird)
3. NTEEV
4. NTEES
5. NTEER

HINT: The answer to 4 is TENSE.

Doggoned Right!

DIRECTIONS

To find the words to an old adage, start with the top word in each column and change one letter as you go down the ladder. The dot in the box shows which letter needs to be changed. Letters do not change position with any move. The Mystery Words at the bottom of the ladders, when solved and unscrambled, will form a well-known saying. Cognitive Chick is holding an extra Mystery Word that is used in the saying, and she has started one ladder to get you going.

Didjaknow... GOOD READING SKILLS ARE ACUTELY ACQUIRED AND REQUIRED

Because today's electronic society is so dependent on printed information, the development and acquisition of good reading skills, learned during the early years, is more important than ever. However, reading, unlike speaking, relies on abilities that must be meticulously taught. To acquire the skill for reading, children must become aware of the relationship between print and sound, and children have to recognize how sounds combine to create words. For example, children must understand that "dog" while spoken and heard as one continuous sound, is actually composed of three letter-sounds that can be rearranged to produce still other words with different sounds and meanings. Dyslexia is the result of impairment in that very phonological ability.

Answer on page 111

A N T	S E T	B U R N	B U T
A N D			
A D D			
A D E			
2	**3**	**4**	**5**

S U N	C R A V E D	H I T C H
6	**7**	**8**

Up A Tree

DIRECTIONS

Arguments begin when one word leads to another, and in this puzzle words not only lead to each other, but often overlap. If you start in slot 1 with the right word and continue clockwise you should have little trouble completing the circle with 18 additional words. Each word starts in a numbered slot that corresponds to the number of the clue.

CLUES

1. Elm, e.g.
2. Marsh plant
3. Redact
4. Tizzy
5. George Michael Cohan's "Over ____"
6. Well-____ (quite knowledgeable)
7. Find the sum
8. Between cube and mince
9. Building material
10. Make a beginning (upon)
11. Brief and pithy
12. Flow gradually
13. Impressively great
14. Ancient of northern Britain
15. Rhythmical stress
16. Employ
17. Char
18. Is for many
19. Soak

Answer on page 111

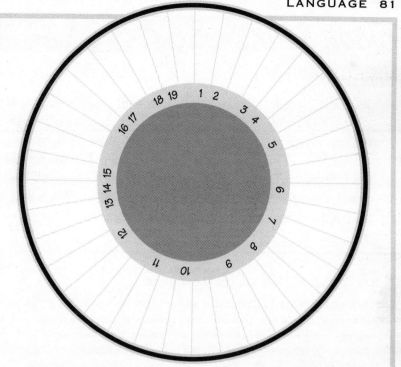

Didjaknow...

LEFT-HANDERS CAN RECOVER LANGUAGE MORE RAPIDLY

After a stroke left-handers often recover language abilities quicker than right-handed women and men, even if those lefties also process language dominantly in their left hemispheres. Left-handers can more easily activate their right-brain processing centres if left-brain language centres are damaged by, for example, a stroke or severe blow. Women normally use both hemispheres anyway, certainly more than men do.

HINT: 15 is ICTUS.

Good Horse Sense

DIRECTIONS

To find the words to an old adage, start with the top word in each column and change one letter as you go down the ladder. The dot in the box shows which letter needs to be changed. Letters do not change position with any move. The Mystery Words at the bottom of the ladders, when solved and unscrambled, will form a well-known saying. Cognitive Chick is holding two extra Mystery Words that are used in the saying, and she has started one ladder to get you going.

Didjaknow... COMPLEX SENTENCES CAN CONFUSE

Read the following: "The dog that mother just fed bit the cat." "Mother just fed the dog that bit the cat." Most likely, you found the first sentence harder to understand. PET scans reveal that complex sentences create a greater load on the frontal lobes where Working Memory is. Although a complicated writing style may ward off dementia because it works the brain, it is best not to confuse readers. When writing or speaking, avoid using sentences that require keeping one idea in mind while reading or hearing another idea in the same sentence.

Answer on page 111

T	O	E
T	O	O
W	O	O
W	H	O

3

R	A	C	E

4

R	O	B	E	D

5

T	I	R	E

6

L	O	O	K	S

7

P	O	I	S	E

8

Jam Session

DIRECTIONS

Arguments begin when one word leads to another, and in this puzzle words not only lead to each other, but often overlap. If you start in slot 1 with the right word and continue clockwise you should have little trouble completing the circle with 17 additional words. Each word starts in a numbered slot that corresponds to the number of the clue.

Didjaknow... DECLARATIVE MEMORY REFERS TO FACTS

The word "memory" commonly refers to conscious, *declarative* memory which involves information and events that are learned, such as

remembering what you did last week, the names of our last six presidents or answers to crossword puzzle clues. Areas of the brain essential for processing this type of memory for words include the hippocampus, amygdala, and cortex surrounding the inner surfaces of the temporal lobe located just above the left

ear. *Non-declarative* memory, such as learned abilities, including skills and habits, is processed in other brain centres.

Answer on page 111

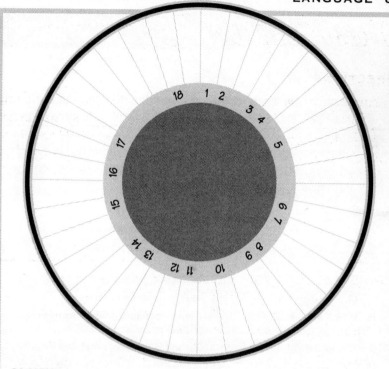

CLUES

1. Fruit preserve
2. Fossil resin
3. European capital
4. Actor Borgnine
5. Cuddle
6. Conducted
7. Rim
8. Precious stone
9. Ant (dial.)
10. Paris subway
11. Between walk and run
12. Helicopter part
13. Pulled apart
14. Excessively adorned
15. Ancient Egyptian deity
16. Flag
17. ___ off (went off the air)
18. ___ vu

Sheep Speak

DIRECTIONS

This puzzle combines anagrams and word hunts. Write out the letters corresponding to the numbers (A=1, B=2, etc.), then rearrange the letters to make a new word that fits the clue. Fill in each square in the grid with its corresponding number and find and circle each of the answers in the grid. Some words are diagonal, and some read from right to left or bottom to top.

CLUES

A.	19 20 1 2 12 5	Manger site produces farm noises
B.	19 20 1 7 8 15 18 14	Male deer plus antler made spook split (two words)
C.	20 9 14 1 21 4 9 15	Metal sound gets tryout
D.	14 15 20 9 1 14	'Tisn't Scottish John, 'tis tribe
E.	1 14 14 1 13 5 19 19	Magnani untidiness leads to sound mind (two words, Lat.)
F.	8 5 9 7 8 20 19	Hills and Everest, comparatively speaking
G.	20 1 18 7 5 20 19	Goals for filmmaker: go after Julia Roberts type (two words)
H.	3 1 18 8 9 14 7 5	Auto door necessity to arrive at card game finale (two words)
I.	1 12 15 14 7 18 5 19 20	Simmered down after an extended interval of silence (two words)
J.	5 18 9 3 1 19 20 15 4	Jong's digit is a matter understood by few
K.	1 12 9 5 14	Foreign dress style (hyph.)
L.	6 18 5 5 23 8 5 5 12 19	Coasts along with comparatively less cads (two words)
M.	19 20 1 18	Preeminent Peter the Great

Answer on page 111

6	13	14	1	18	20	19	15	8	7
16	5	19	15	20	5	18	9	3	1
7	14	23	20	9	8	7	14	15	1
5	19	5	5	2	9	9	10	12	21
20	19	14	23	18	7	14	9	19	4
19	1	9	20	8	8	14	7	20	20
20	14	19	3	20	5	5	15	1	9
1	1	1	15	21	19	18	5	5	15
18	5	7	14	1	20	19	15	12	14
18	14	15	9	20	1	14	7	2	19

N. 23 9 14 5 19 — Clarets give you strength

O. 19 9 14 14 5 18 — Wrongdoer lands some shots next to the bull's-eye

P. 1 20 20 21 — Aleutian island gets tense

Q. 20 15 18 20 — Legally wrong pace

R. 9 19 8 20 1 — Divine form states archaically

CITATIONS:

P. 72 Denckla, Martha Bridge, MD, Director, Developmental Cognitive Neurology, The Johns Hopkins School of Medicine. From a Presentation at Science of Cognition Conference, Library of Congress, Washington, D.C., 6 Oct. 1999.

P. 74, 76, 81 (2001) The Brainwaves Center, Bass River, MA.

P. 78 Eden, Guinevere D. Phil., Georgetown University Medical Center. From a presentation at Science of Cognition Conference, Library of Congress, Washington, D.C., 6 Oct. 1999.

P. 82, 76 Stromswold, K. et al. (1996). Localization of syntactic comprehension by Positron Emission Tomography. Brain and Language 52:452-73; Snowden, D. S. et al. (1996). Linguistic ability in early life and cognitive function and Alzheimer's disease in late life. Journal of the American Medical Association 275/7:528-32.

P. 84 Squire, Larry R. PhD, Research Career Scientist, VA Medical Center, San Diego; Professor of Psychiatry and Neuroscience, University of California-San Diego School of Medicine. From a Presentation at the Science of Cognition Conference, Library of Congress, Washington, D. C., 6 Oct. 1999.

Section Six
SOCIAL-EMOTIONAL

Consciousness in humans is awareness of emotions. Emotions are the exposed tips of responses to sub-conscious survival-needs that our primitive brain systems pick up — immediate danger, opportunities to reproduce, sources of food. Humans can become consciously aware of some of their body's automatic reactions set in motion by unconscious responses to basic survival stimuli. The human animal may be unique in its ability to see itself as a player in the primitive drama of survival. It can then control its emotional reactions, sometimes, with an eye to future benefit. In his book "The Feeling of What Happens", Antonio R. Damasio calls that self-awareness "consciousness". The title draws a line in the sand. On one side stands the neuroscientific study of the human nervous system as it alerts and signals and responds body-wide. On the other, stands the philosophical or religious approach to human consciousness which tends to attribute something *that* uniquely influential to a specific organ or ephemeral beyond the biological realm.

When the brain becomes aware of any passing data it considers to be "survival-quality", it releases hormones and neurotransmitters that cause increased heart rate, eye dilation, trembling, goose bumps, and many other physical changes we are, and are not, conscious of. What self-awareness there is takes place in the cortex, mostly the front part over the eyes, an area that allows humans to plan ahead and cooperate in social groups. The gift of the frontal part of the human cortex is awareness of how the more primitive part of the brain is responding. That awareness allows humans to control their primitive responses for long-term benefit without sacrificing short-term safety. Don't worry, if the danger is imminently life-threatening, the cortex never hears about it;

the primitive brain systems freeze you or start you running without your even being aware of anything. The brain needs only nanoseconds to transmit a signal, such as "tyrannosaurus rex there", from the primitive limbic system to the cortex, and wait while the cortex checks past experience to make sure it is not just a cloud formation so you can go on picking bananas before it is too dark. Even so, the limbic system reacts first and leaves the thinking until later on the principal that if you stop to remember the name of something as big as a "tyrannosaurus" it is too late. Yes, emotions can get humans into trouble — from constant stress responses to a bad marriage — but survival has always been the tradeoff.

The human cortex's role in restricting the expression of emotions allows people to get along with each other, for one thing. They can then achieve long-term goals that allow them to survive. Thanks to self-awareness, individuals can choose to put limitations on their personal advantage for the protection they reap from long-term social support. Perhaps guilt is the downside of that "gift" of self-awareness. On the other hand, remorseless sociopaths often turn out to have suffered damage to the same part of the prefrontal cortex that controls emotions in favour of the future fruits of social cooperation.

We find it difficult to devise pencil-on-paper exercises for such subject matter. Appropriate emotional response and effective social interaction present moving targets that true-false and multiple choice cannot hit. This section, therefore, offers mental exercises that two people can do together. It provides scientific findings about gender differences in the human brain and it offers self-tests, one of which asks you to compare your ethics with those of business school graduates and convicted felons.

DIRECTIONS

This one will be more fun if you work on it with another person. It presents two interesting challenges. The first part will show bias in how you think. The second will test your ability to recognize social needs and accurately link images with the appropriate need.

The symbols on the facing page were designed for the Olympic Games. Your first challenge is to pair each symbol with one other symbol in ways you find most compellingly significant. There is no "correct" solution, but how you choose to pair them will reveal whether your dominant skill is convergent, inside-the-envelope logic or divergent, outside-the-envelope creative flexibility.

Your second challenge is to identify the message each symbol was originally designed to deliver as used in the venue of the Olympic Games. Try to come up with only one-or two-word answers. If you are design-savvy or an Olympic sports aficionado, see how close you can come to naming the host nation for which these were designed and the year they were used. There are correct answers to the two parts of this second challenge.

Didjaknow... INFANTS ARE AMBIDEXTROUS

All newborns will reach for a reward with the nearest hand. Even if an infant usually grabs with her right hand, if you place an object left of midline, she will grab with her left. Even if her left hand is restrained, she still will not reach with her far right hand. This is normal infant behaviour. It does not mean your child will grow up to be ambidextrous. Only after a child begins walking, can a parent conclude whether a child is left- or right-handed.

Answer on page 112

Downside of Downsizing

In a recent study, inmates in three minimum-security prisons were presented with the ethical issues contained in the questions that follow. The same questions were posed to students in business courses at a dozen universities. The answer section compares the way MBA students and inmates responded. How do your answers compare with the responses of the two groups?

Mr. Stern is a long-time, faithful employee of your company. He works in the sales department of the computer test equipment division, where his job is to locate used test equipment that hi-tech companies are willing to part with, negotiate a price, and pass the equipment on to the engineering department for refurbishment and resale.

Mr. Stern used to be one of your company's top sales executives, but lately his productivity has been slipping. For the last two years, his monthly commissions have been lower than those of most of the younger account executives in the sales department, lower even than some of the brand-new sales employees. Part of the problem may be that at his age — 62 — Mr. Stern just might not relate very well to the young computer engineers in the hi-tech companies he's dealing with. His territory also has a fair amount of ethnic diversity, and it might not be a bad idea to add more minority members to the sales department staff. (Mr. Stern is white.) While he is still a faithful and diligent employee, the feeling among upper management is that Mr. Stern is no longer worth his base salary.

What would you do if you were told by your superior to pressure Mr. Stern into early retirement in order to:

Answer on page 112

   i. make room for a younger employee
  ii. make room for a member of a minority race, or
iii. save the firm the cost of full benefits

i.
(A) Just do it.
(B) Object, but still do it.
(C) Transfer or demote the employee, but don't fire him.
(D) Suggest early retirement to the employee, but don't pressure him.
(E) Just not do it — it's not right.
(F) Just not do it — it's not my job, or there might be legal problems.

ii.
(A) Just do it.
(B) Object, but still do it.
(C) Transfer or demote the employee, but don't fire him.
(D) Suggest early retirement to the employee, but don't pressure him.
(E) Just not do it — it's not right.
(F) Just not do it — it's not my job, or there might be legal problems..

iii.
(A) Just do it.
(B) Object, but still do it.
(C) Transfer or demote the employee, but don't fire him.
(D) Suggest early retirement to the employee, but don't pressure him.
(E) Just not do it — it's not right.
(F) Just not do it — it's not my job, or there might be legal problems.

Hypnotizability

People who are most likely to create false memories in response to misinformation tend to score higher in tests that rate their ability to produce vivid visual imagery on demand, are likely to be hypnotized more easily and to show a greater need for social approval.

For this self-test, you will need a helper to play the role of "hypnotist" by slowly reading the following segments of text aloud as you concentrate with your eyes closed on what you hear.

PART ONE

Read this aloud:

"For this first part, please close your eyes and sit in a relaxed position. Place your left hand in your lap with the palm facing up. Imagine that Novocaine is being injected into the little finger of your left hand. You feel the slight prick of the needle in the tip of your little finger and then your finger starts to tingle the same as when you sleep on your arm or when some part of your body falls asleep. You feel your little finger tingle, and then you feel the very tip start to go numb. Imagine the Novocaine moving up your finger, as first the tip goes numb, and then the first knuckle, and then the second knuckle, and then your whole little finger is numb all the way to where it meets your hand. Now, the whole little finger on your left hand is completely numb, like a fat lump of clay.

"Now imagine the Novocaine moving into your next finger, the ring finger, as it starts to feel numb as well. Tell yourself that this next finger is feeling number and number, until it too feels like a lump of clay, or a fat piece of rubber. Now, both fingers are numb, fat, and rubbery.

"Now, bend your thumb over and feel the two fingers at the other end of your hand. Those fingers are so numb that they can't really feel the thumb touching them, just a dull sensation of pressure.

"Now, tell yourself you've just imagined the whole thing, and your fingers feel perfectly normal, and not numb at all, and you can feel sensations in them perfectly fine."

PART TWO

"For this part, lie down. Keep your eyes closed as you listen to the instructions. Imagine yourself lying by a lake in Northern Italy. There's a carpet of warm, fragrant grass beneath you. It's a beautiful summer day, with a warm sun shining out of a robin's-egg-blue sky. A gentle breeze caresses your face. Picture the blue sky with a few small, cottony clouds floating slowly by, and feel the warm sun on your face and neck. In the distance you hear a small child laugh.

"Feel the gentle warmth of the sun soothe your shoulders and chest as you lie on the soft grass. The breeze caresses the backs of your hands, and then you notice how warm and pleasant the sun feels on them. Your shoulders, arms, and hands feel so relaxed in the warm sun and gentle breeze. Small, brightly-coloured sailboats drift lazily on the blue lake.

"Tell yourself that you've never felt so relaxed, as the warmth of the sun flows down your arm and through your fingers, down your chest to your stomach and legs. Just let yourself go limp. The smell of the warm grass is so relaxing, so soothing. Let yourself feel the warmth of the sun as every muscle in your body melts into complete relaxation. Even your toes feel warm, calm, at peace with the grass, the water lapping at the lake's shore, the blue sky, the universe. Just let yourself feel calm, relaxed, so lazy you might never get up.

"Now, open your eyes and let yourself continue to feel relaxed, but awake and alert at the same time. You may get up if you wish."

Didjaknow... **YOU'LL HAVE AN EDGE IF YOU STAND TO HIS LEFT IN A FACE-TO-FACE**

Next time your boss calls you into his office to debate a work issue, try sitting or standing to the left side of him. Being in his left visual field forces your boss's brain to use its right side first, before passing it over to his left hemisphere where language is normally processed. Why would this give you an edge? For most people, the hemisphere on the right side of the brain is literal — more likely to take action than compare incoming data with past experience. Therefore your boss's first impression is less likely to be analytical and so it will be less judgmental. Remember, in face-to-face confrontation, move to the left of the person you are going up against.

SCORING:

1. In the first part, you were asked to imagine that first your little finger and then the second finger on your left hand were turning numb from a shot of Novocaine. Compared to what you would have felt if your finger really had been injected with Novocaine, what you felt was:

> Not at all the same (0 pt.)
> A little the same (1 pt.)
> Somewhat the same (2 pts.)
> Much the same (3 pts.)
> Exactly the same (4 pts.)

2. In the second part, you were asked to imagine that you were lying by a peaceful Italian lake, with a warm sun and gentle breeze making you feel completely relaxed. Compared to what you would have felt if you really had been relaxing by an Italian lake, what you felt was:

> Not at all the same (0 pt.)
> A little the same (1 pt.)
> Somewhat the same (2 pts.)
> Much the same (3 pts.)
> Exactly the same (4 pts.)

Totals: 0-3 pts.: Low hypnotizability
4-6 pts.: Average hypnotizability
7-8 pts.: High hypnotizability

Significant Other Differences

ANATOMICAL DIFFERENCES

The human brain is composed of three major components: grey matter, where computation takes place, consists of nerve cells, dendrites, and axons; white matter, called myelin, that acts like insulation for the "wires" that grey matter uses to communicate from one region to another; and cerebrospinal fluid. While females have a smaller cranium than males (1200cc versus 1400cc), they have the same amount of grey matter as men. As cranial volume increases, men show a proportionate increase in grey and white matter, but women show a disproportionate increase: 50 percent of a male brain is grey matter, but 55 percent of the female brain will be grey matter. Why? Because woman's smaller cranium adapts by packing more neurons into it and, because there is less space, less white matter is needed to protect the "wires" since the neurons have a shorter distance to travel.

DIFFERENCES IN RESPONSE TIME

It is common knowledge that men tend to be physically bigger than women, but males also have the ability to execute motor commands quicker and more accurately than females. When asked to tap a finger during a battery of motor function tests, it was found that men could tap their fingers much faster than women. A light beam measured the tapping to ensure the difference had nothing to do with muscle strength. Moreover, PET scan studies show the cerebellum is more active in men and, since this is the area of the brain having to do with motor skills, it helps explain why men excel on tests involving motor function.

DIFFERENCE IN FOCUS

Male and female brains were studied by FMRI (function magnetic resonance imaging) while performing spatial and language tests. For both sexes, the imaging revealed a greater increase of activity in the left hemisphere for verbal problems, relative to greater increase in the right hemisphere for spatial tasks. Women appear to recruit both sides of the brain for both tasks, i.e., their brains literally race all over the place to recall an answer. This may be an advantage for some tasks. As verbal tests get harder, more regions need to be searched to find the answer. But using both hemispheres puts women at a disadvantage for spatial tasks. Because one part (the right hemisphere) of men's brains is specialized to perform spatial tasks, they perform better for that reason than women who lack a specialized area for spatial processing.

WOMEN REMEMBER VISUAL DETAILS BETTER

If you want the real lowdown on what the Jones's house looks like, it's best to ask a woman because recent tests show that women exhibit a greater visual memory than men. A group of men and women were asked to carefully study a picture of a roomful of furniture for one minute. They were then given a picture of an empty room and shown various pieces of furniture. Asked if various pieces of furniture had been in the room and, if so, where they had been situated, women remembered the items and where they were placed much better than men.

DIFFERENCES IN CONTROLLING EMOTIONAL IMPULSES

After the age of 40, men begin to lose that part of the brain that says, "Stop and think about the consequences!" Besides being responsible for abstraction, mental flexibility and attention, the frontal lobe also plays the role of the inhibiter. It is intimately connected to the limbic system, which is the emotional part of the brain, but the relationship between the two is reciprocal. While the emotional part of the brain may say, "Let's, do it", the frontal part will respond: "Wait! Think of the outcome!" Young men have larger frontal lobes than women, proportionate to body size, but after the age of 40, a man's frontal lobe will begin to shrink. A woman's frontal lobe, however, does not shrink with age.

BOTH MEN AND WOMEN HAVE TWO EMOTIONAL BRAINS ...

The emotional or limbic brain can be divided into two sub-systems located deep within the centre of the brain: the limbic system and, below that, the "older" reptilian response system. This old  limbic system reacts to emotion through action, and because evolution does not throw anything away, this part still exists deep in the human brain. The second part of the emotional brain lies above it, in the cingulate gyrus of the cortex. The cingulate gyrus is new in evolutionary terms and evolved along with the brain's vocal and language areas. The new limbic system provides ways to modulate emotion by expressing it through language, making humans the only species on earth who can both act out and verbalize emotion.

... BUT THE "OLD" LIMBIC BRAIN IS MORE ACTIVE IN MEN

There's a big difference in the way men and women handle emotion, and this is especially true when they become angry. Read any newspaper and it becomes obvious that when it comes to acts of violence and aggression, men win hands down. The likelihood that a murder is committed by a man is 40,000:1 and this phenomenon is seen all over the world. It's not due to physical strength alone — firearms equalize this factor since it doesn't takes much strength to pull a trigger. While men may show anger in an aggressive, physical manner, women tend to be verbal. Men fight. Women talk it over.

EMOTIONS ARE KEY TO SURVIVAL FOR BOTH MEN AND WOMEN

There are six emotions that can be reliably detected on the human face in every culture around the world — and detecting emotion in others is a key element in the survival game. The six emotions are anger, fear, sadness, disgust, surprise and happiness. Lower species, such as crocodiles and rats, do not smile. Therefore, happiness or a sense of humour is recognized as a fairly new emotion in the evolutionary scale. Happiness is the only positive emotion displayed on the human face; no other is seen. Because the evolutionary process has shown that it is more important for the survival of a species to show negative emotions, this will explain why humans display five negative emotions and only one positive.

WOMEN ARE QUICKER AND MORE ACCURATE AT DETECTING EMOTIONS

When a face is computer-morphed into the shape of vase, a woman can tell whether it is happy or sad in 30 milliseconds. It will take her 20 milliseconds more to decide whether the image is a face or a vase. Men, on the other hand, take longer to attach an emotion to the image. Moreover, PET scan studies have shown that women did not have to activate much of their brain to gauge the correct facial emotion. And even though a man takes longer, and activates more of his brain to identify an emotion, he is still less likely to come up with the correct answer.

FEAR IS AN EMOTION MUCH MORE EASILY DETECTED BY WOMEN

 There is a dramatic difference in the way men and women detect the facial expression of fear. And when men feel real fear, rather than posing with a fearful expression, women can detect the truly felt emotion much more easily. Men had a harder time identifying fear in other men, even when the man observed was actually feeling fear. And when a woman is the one expressing fear, the same result is even greater: men have a much harder time differentiating a woman's truly evoked fear from a posed fear.

MEN CAN TELL WHEN A WOMAN IS HAPPY MUCH MORE EASILY THAN WHEN SHE IS SAD

Emotional discrimination tests given to groups of men and women showed one striking similarity: women are more sensitive to happy and sad emotions expressed on the faces of men than of women. Men are also more sensitive to emotions expressed on a man's face. However, men find it more difficult to detect sadness on the faces of women. Although men are more likely to detect real sadness than a false expression of sadness, if you're a woman you cannot take it for granted that your man can always tell if you're sad just by looking at your face.

CITATIONS

P. 92 Diamond, Adele (1999). Learning and the Brain Conference, Boston, MA.
   November 7-9.

P. 96 Drake, R.A. and Binghamm, B.R. (1985). Induced lateral orientation and
   persuasibility. Brain Cognition 4:156-64.

   Drake, R. A. (1991). Processing persuasive arguments: recall and recognition as
   a function of agreement and manipulated activation asymmetry. Brain Cognition
   15/1:83-94.

P. 98-105 Gur, Rubin C. (1999). Sex Differences in Learning. From a presentation at
   the Learning and the Brain Conference, Boston, MA. Nov. 7-9.

Solutions

```
        1
        E
   2        2
    E  V  E
 1            1
  E  V  A  V  E
   2        2
    E  V  E
        E
        1
```

ADAM & EVA? P. 12

The only positive, one possibility statement was Dick's. The others were guessing.

THE ABLE ACCOUNTANT P. 14

15	6	9	4
10	3	16	5
8	13	2	11
1	12	7	14

THIRTY-FOUR ALL P. 16

1	9	6	1	4
3	6	1	1	9
2	8	9	1	7
2	5	6	1	6
3	2	4	1	8

In each horizontal row, the three digit number at the left is the square of the two-digit number at the right. The square root of 324 is 18.

THE SQUARE ROOTER P. 22

2	1	+	3	6	=	5	7
	9	x	6	+ 3	=	5	7
	8	x	8	- 7	=	5	7
	9	x	8	- 1 5	=	5	7
2	9	x	2	- 1	=	5	7
4	4	+	1	8 - 5	=	5	7

ANGRY*!$%?TYPIST P. 24

108 BRAIN-BUILDING GAMES

SECTION TWO: MEMORY

EARLY EARLY BIRD P. 26

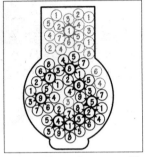

CIRCLES WITHIN CIRCLES P. 28

1	2 7	8	3 9	
4 7	1		5 1	6 6
7 9	4		8 9	6
9		9 1	2	1
	10 1	7	9	8

FRENCH CONNECTION P. 30

Theme Word:
MUSIC

1. Miles Davis
2. Mary Martin
3. Martha Graham
4. Thelonious Monk
5. Franz Schubert
6. Claude Debussy
7. Johann Strauss
8. Roger Sessions
9. Jasha Heifetz
10. Leonard Bernstein
11. Gioacchino Rossini
12. Enrico Caruso
13. Hoagy Carmichael
14. Aaron Copland

HEAVENLY HARMONIES P. 32

SECTION THREE: COMPUTATION

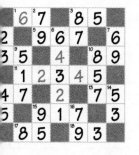

6	7		8	5	
2		9	6	7	6
3	5		4	8	9
	1	2	3	4	5
4	7		2	7	5
5		9	1	7	3
	8	5		9	3

ADD-VENTURE PLUS P. 38

	1	4		3	2	
7		8	9	6		7
6	8		7		9	8
	3	4	5	6	8	
9	6		6		6	2
4		4	8	6		8
	9	8		8	4	

ADDENDUM & EVE P. 40

	5	6	7	8	9	
4	8	3		9	8	3
6	7	8	9		7	5
7		9	6	5		8
8	5		3	8	6	7
9	6	7		7	4	9
	7	9	6	3	5	

ADDICTIVE PLEASURES P. 42

9	7	5	3	6		7
5	1	8	6		9	4
8	6		5	3	1	2
6	2		7	5	8	
4		9	4	2		9
	7	8			7	8
		6	9	4	8	2

TOT UP & TALLY HO! P. 44

Start by solving 1 Across, 4 Down and 6 Down, 1 Down and 10 Across. The prime number in 8 Across is 661; the prime numbers in 9 Across are 5 and 13.

8	1			4	5
4		5	3	2	1
	8	4	6	2	
7	9	3	2		
6	5			4	9

SQUARE DANCES P. 46

1 Across calls for the smallest possible odd number that will produce a two-digit square: 5.

	2	5		
3	1	2	1	
6	6	9		1
	1	1	2	4
4	9		6	4

3 Across is the three digit square of 11. 3 down gives you the beginning of 4 Across, which is then easy to complete. 5 Down and 7 Down give you all the info needed to complete the puzzle.

PRIME TIME P. 48

The consecutive numbers can't go higher than 7....6 ; this series, however, would result in 8's and would therefore be incorrect for 6 Down. 5 Across refers to a Heinz product. 8 Across is the square of 4, which in turn is the square of 2. 2 Down is the square of 16. 6 Down is the square of 25.

1	2	3	4	5
	5	7		1
6	6	6	6	6
2		1	6	
5	4	3	2	1

ROOT CAUSES P. 50

Fill in the obvious first: 1 Across, 6 Across, the first three digits of 8 Across, all of 2 Down and 3 Down. At 7 Across the largest factor of 56 is 28, half is 14, which squared gives you 7 Down. You now have completed 1 Down and you know the prime number is 41. This enables you to complete 5 Down and 10 Across.

1	7	5	1		
6	7	6			1
8	1		7	1	4
1	1	1	9	4	
	1	7	6	4	

CALCULATED SURPRISES P. 52

SECTION FOUR: SPATIAL

The interior design of the room and clothing of the adult parents are both made up of rectangles. The drawing their son is showing them is a curved line, implying that his values are "out of line" with theirs.

CIRCLING THE SQUARE P. 58

Here are six of the many possible solutions. In each square the arrangement of each colour — black, grey, and white — represents a solution.

DRAUGHTBOARD SQUARE P. 60

Dick knew the name of the town they had just been through, it was one of those on the signpost, and was able to orient both the sign and himself. (He also took over the driving.)

UNEXPECTED WINDFALL P. 62

TOPSY-TURVEY TANGRAMS P. 64

Answer: 9

2

TWICE BURNED P. 66

SECTION FIVE: LANGUAGE

S	T	R	A	P
T	R	A	S	H
R	A	D	I	O
A	S	I	A	N
P	H	O	N	Y

WATCH PARTS P. 72

Winner-Word
PUZZLE   TOTAL 1010

SEXUAL
AXLES
RELAXED PI
ALE LAX PIE
ZEAL AX RIPE
LAZED A PRIZE
DAZZLE PRIZED

WINNER-WORD P. 74

C	R	E	T	E
R	A	V	E	N
E	V	E	N	T
T	E	N	S	E
E	N	T	E	R

ERECT AN ISLAND P. 76

ANT	SET	BURN	BUT
AND	GET	BORN	BIT
ADD	GUT	BORE	BIN
ADE	BUT	BARE	TIN
ODE	BET	CARE	TON
ODD	NET	CART	YON
OLD	NEW	CANT	YOU

SUN	CRAVED	HITCH
SON	BRAVED	HUTCH
TON	BRACED	HUNCH
TOE	TRACED	BUNCH
FOE	TRACES	BENCH
DOE	TRACKS	BEACH
DOG	TRICKS	TEACH

DOGGONED RIGHT P. 78

UP A TREE P. 80

TOE	RACE	ROBED
TOO	LACE	ROWED
WOO	LACK	SOWED
WHO	LOCK	SEWED
WHY	BOCK	SEWER
THY	BOOK	SEVER
THE	LOOK	NEVER

TIRE	LOOKS	POISE
TIME	BOOKS	NOISE
LIME	BOOTS	NOOSE
LIFE	BOOTH	MOOSE
RIFE	SOOTH	MOUSE
RIFT	SOUTH	HOUSE
GIFT	MOUTH	HORSE

GOOD HORSE SENSE P. 82

JAM SESSION P. 84

SHEEP SPEAK P. 86

A. STABLE/BLEATS
B. STAG HORN/GHOST RAN
C. TIN AUDIO/AUDITION
D. NOT IAN/NATION
E. ANNA MESS/MENS SANA
F. HEIGHTS/HIGHEST
G. TARGETS/GET STAR
H. CAR HINGE/REACH GIN
I. LONG REST/LOST ANGER
J. ERICA'S TOE/ESOTERICA
K. ALIEN/A-LINE
L. FREEWHEELS/FEWER HEELS
M. STAR/TSAR
N. WINES/SINEW
O. SINNER/INNERS
P. ATTU/TAUT
Q. TORT/TROT
R. ISHTA/SAITH

SECTION SIX: SOCIAL/EMOTIONAL

> **Olympic Games, Mexico, 1968**
> Row 1: Telephone; Mail; Currency Exchange; First Aid
> Row 2: Toilets, Men; Toilets, Women; Information; Bus
> Row 3: Restaurant; Coffee Shop; Shops; No Smoking
> Row 4: Smoking; Locker; Shower; Press
> Row 5: Track & Field; Football; Swimming; Gymnastics

OUTSIDE THE ENVELOPE P. 92

> Answers are expressed as a percent response by MBA students and inmates respectively. Where the numbers don't add up to 100, other options such as "don't know" were chosen.

	MBA Students	Inmates		MBA Students	Inmates		MBA Students	Inmates
i.	(A) 22.5	(A) 46.3	ii.	(A) 19.1	(A) 23.2	iii.	(A) 14.9	(A) 13.6
	(B) 3.0	(B) 9.1		(B) 2.8	(B) 11.7		(B) 3.4	(B) 4.5
	(C) 18.6	(C) 10.6		(C) 17.5	(C) 11.1		(C) 17.0	(C) 9.1
	(D) 26.4	(D) 20.3		(D) 25	(D) 31.1		(D) 20.5	(D) 31.8
	(E) 15.4	(E) 4.5		(E) 19.8	(E) 13.6		(E) 25.5	(E) 25.2
	(F) 7.6	(F) 4.5		(F) 8.7	(F) 4.6		(F) 9.2	(F) 11.1

DOWNSIDE OF DOWNSIZING P. 94